sensual austerity

by Maxine Bristow

CONTENTS

18 x 51 over 11.44, 2002
Overall dimensions: H214cmxW 1114cm
Individual pieces: H214cmxW51cm
Photography: Sara Morris

INTRODUCTION

sensual austerity is a new installation of work and other related interventions by the artist Maxine Bristow. Her interest as a fine artist, researcher and educator focuses on textile practice and its place and meaning in visual culture. Her work may be described as 'minimalist': this suggestion is confounded by complexity and a richness in detail. Bristow seeks to subvert our expectations through the use of forms 'tailored' and explored in the spaces we normally take for granted. She uses 'accepted' textile traditions to find new ways of enabling us to see the world anew. She confounds the demeaning stereotype that needlework and plain sewing are trivial 'women's work' creating new perspectives using traditional methods to construct other ways of thinking about textile practice.

Bristow's ideas have often been articulated in a series of large scale, cloth constructed, gesso encrusted 'bag' forms seen 'head on' in the same manner as a painting on a gallery wall. More recent work is concerned with what she describes as the 'poetics' and 'politics' of space and our engagement with it. She expects that we, the viewers, will not be passive but think about what we see, about our bodily engagement with space, and in particular about those features of the built environment such as light-switches, handles, handrails, etc, with which we have an actual physical, though often unnoticed, relationship.

sensual austerity is richly sensual and there is the nub of matter: the contradiction we seek to resolve – the struggle between reason and emotion.

Phil Cosker
Hub Director

1,452: not motif but ground.1998
Overall dimensions: H130cmxW420cm
Individual pieces: H130cmxW120cm
Photography: Dewi Tannatt Lloyd

3x19: Intersecting a Seam. 1999
Overall dimensions: H163cmxW418cm
Individual pieces:H163cmxW124cm
Photography: Dewi Tannatt Lloyd

ARTICULATE SILENCE
AN OVERVIEW OF THE WORK OF MAXINE BRISTOW

by Elisa Oliver

"If it is true of human beings that language enables us to be where we are not, and prevents us from ever being anywhere but beside ourselves, then it is the voice that stretches us out between here and elsewhere. One cannot be fully 'here' unless one is silent; one cannot vocalise without being 'there' as well as here, without being drawn out into the ambivalence of being here and there at once". (Steven Connor)[1]

Maxine Bristow's work is permeated by ambiguity, silent but speaking volumes. Having taken both undergraduate and postgraduate courses in textiles at Manchester Metropolitan University, Bristow emerged in 1985 with a practice that clearly engaged with both the context and practice of the history of textiles. However her work resonates with such a range of references that such a straight-forward categorisation soon becomes impossible.

Born in the North West Bristow was both physically and emotionally surrounded by the textile industry; the physical, transforming architecture of the cotton industry and a family heritage of plain, functional sewing passed down from her grandmother. Interestingly both architectural space and domestic labour have become features of her work, absorbed and transformed in a manner that both continues and pushes at the boundaries of textile art but in a subtle, almost silent way.

After graduating Bristow worked as a freelance designer and then in 1989 took up a part time teaching post in the fine art department at the University of Chester, as a textile specialist. The proximity to fine art and the contradictions between selling and teaching were to have an ongoing influence on the work.

We can see this emerge in the body of work exhibited in 1997 in shows such as *Flexible*, touring from the Netherlands. These shows see the early

trademark bags, shown in series, in muted grey fabrics distressed through the application of gesso. They have in their repetition and physicality an affinity with Minimalism and debates on objecthood, something happily acknowledged by Bristow.[2] The bags hybrid state between textile, sculpture and painting reflect her awareness, consolidated through teaching, of the limits and artificiality of categories such as craft and fine art, and the equally limiting void between the commercial and the creative process of making.

These concerns and their trajectories are battled out in the works but with a muffled quietude that gives them a very particular presence. The tradition of plain sewing asserts itself in the meticulously sewn, bound buttonholes that recur as a serial motif. Functionless, like the bags themselves, they possess, in this redundant gesture both the effacement of a particular type of labour and, from the perspective of the post-industrial present, a melancholic sense of loss. This collapsing of past into present creates a type of stasis that while appearing to silence both temporalities is in fact what ultimately makes them articulate. The aesthetic of Minimalism resonates against the very post-modern condition of empty repetition, we are forever in the moment but, with the past always in reach, we appear locked in an endless oscillation between the two. For many this has created an 'endgame' situation, however, ironically it is the blind repetition of the useless buttonhole and the gaping void of the bag that facilitates the return of lost voices, articulates present ones and realises a sense of transformation, as the labour of textile work is reinstated and reinvigorated through its circulation in a whole new context of debate. The work stands as both witness to the past and chronicler of the present.

From 1997 into 2000 Bristow continued to exhibit nationally and internationally in shows such as *Textures of Memory: The Poetics of Cloth* at Angel Row Nottingham in 1999 and *The Contemplative Stitch* at the Kansas City Art Institute, USA in 2000. While these shows continued to place the work in a predominately textile context the work itself increasingly aligned itself with key debates within fine art. In particular an

Installation shot, Jerwood Applied Arts Prize 2002: Textiles
Includes:
Needlepoint: ref no. 7510, 3 x 63cm surround,
18 x 51 over 11.44
Darn: ref no. 648, 3 x 146 cm division

interest in the social construction of and engagement with space, at this point a preoccupation for artists and theorists in extrapolating ideas of gender and definitions of place.[3] Reflecting on the way the bags articulated the space of the gallery and imposed a bodily, perceptual experience in the viewer Bristow began to pull together a range of gestating ideas.

As early as 1997 Bristow had made a casual observation while in the gym that the functional details of institutional architecture bore a strong visual correlation to the quiet, repetitive motifs of the bags. At this point she made a mould of a light switch filling the functional switch with grey blanket.[4] By 2004 this had evolved into a body of work that tested her interests in new ways.

Through the Surface, Collaborative Textile Artists from Britain and Japan 2004/2005 (touring) had provided an opportunity to reflect on work to date and as a mentoring exchange project allow debate and collaboration to help forward this, a contrast to the isolation of the studio. The work produced continued the concern with series and repetition seen in the bags. However the motif changed, rows of moulded light switches their switch replaced with minute needlepoint, handrails and crowd barriers also visited by the needle began to emerge. The nature of touch, implicit whenever textile is present, and the bodily presence of the bags also remains but is further translated into that of gesture, in this case a gesture so small, the switching of a light, that the tension between silence and voice is again articulated. Such gestures, particularly evident in the handrails, are so small that they are almost unconscious mediators of self, spatial regulators that once we become aware of them bring into question the very notion of boundary and in their silence the political construction of the visible and the invisible. In this context the work also addresses and brings voice through the banal, in the over-familiar and everyday quality of both the gesture and the object that while muted speaks volumes.

12

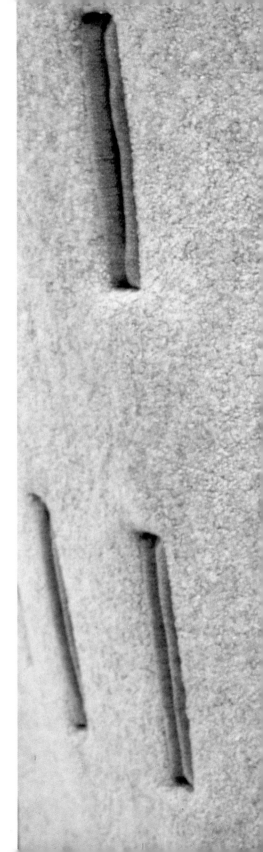

Square Correlation No. 51999[Detail]
Dimensions: H74cmxW150cm
Photography: Sara Morris

The longer you spend with these pieces and witness their utilisation of theories of space and the everyday the more insistent that voice becomes. On one level this emerges through the uncanny,[5] that means by which the familiar becomes unfamiliar and seen in equivalent artists work such as the upholstered protrusions of Nina Saunders.[6] The bags also engaged with the uncanny but it is the greater familiarity of the light switches, conduits and crowd barriers that make it more overt in these later works. Defined as the return of the repressed, the uncanny, could in these works be identified as the return or voicing of silenced women. Additionally the works referencing of modernism in their Minimalist and serialised form seen in conjunction with a sense of return and the past reflects the popular definition of Post-modern nostalgia as the return of Modernism's repressed.[7] However nostalgia here relates not to a reactionary desire to reinstate the past but to a need to vocalise and hence politicise those that have been silenced.

Equally, the everyday and banal quality of the work taps away at a peripheral vision so insistently that it begins to usurp the centre. The selected architectural features cross that strange hinterland between the known and the anonymous, institutional architecture that is both immediately recognizable and endlessly reproducible, underlining a sense of self at the same time that it obliterates it. As such, while small and potentially overlooked such features become impossible to ignore. Rather than effacing self these works demand a different and more insistent type of perception. In such 'non-places'.[8]

"new kind of seeing subject exists, a kind of mutant: one who sees itself looking from the vantage point of being nowhere and elsewhere simultaneously. What the viewer confronts in every non-place is an image of self: the only face to be seen, the only voice to be heard, is one's own, yet echoed by millions of others in other non-places". (Soo Jin Kim)[9]

The banality of the objects takes us in some ways to the limit of perception, but rather than becoming silent they become a marker of cognition of self-awareness. In this way they become charged with a new potential, to quote Soo Jin again,

14

LEFT
Kit for production of Needlepoint:
ref no. 7510, 3 x 63cm surround, 2001
H58cm x W36cm
Photography: Maxine Bristow

RIGHT
Installation shot, Jerwood Applied Arts Prize 2002: Textiles
Includes:
Needlepoint: ref no. 7510, 3 x 63cm surround,
Photography: Maxine Bristow

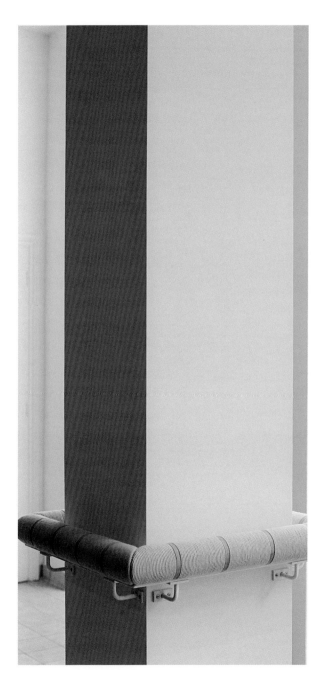

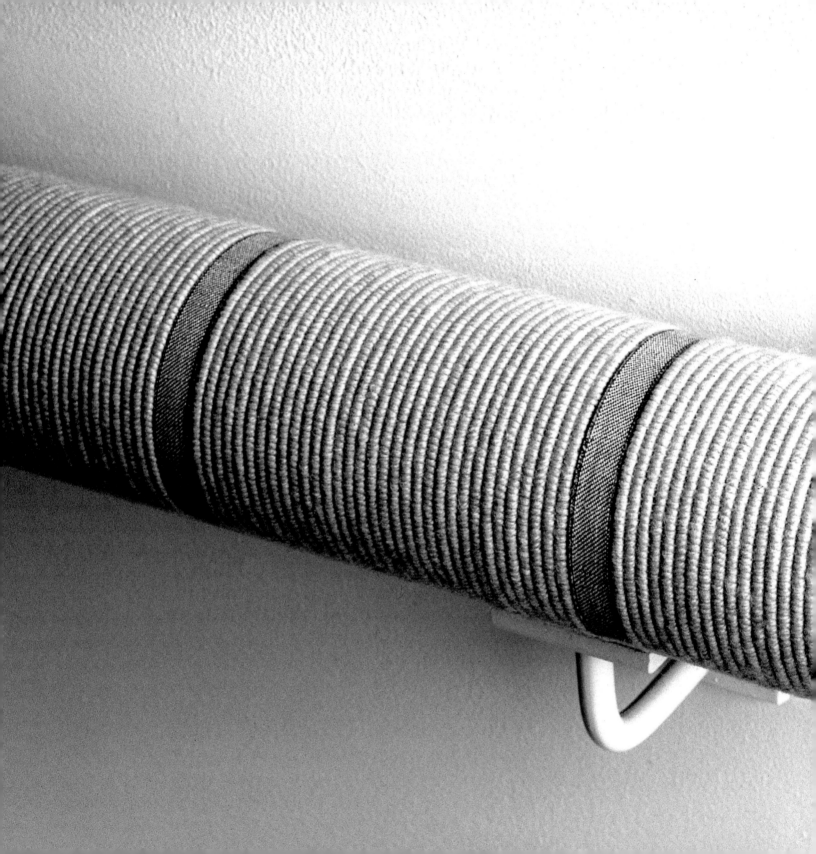

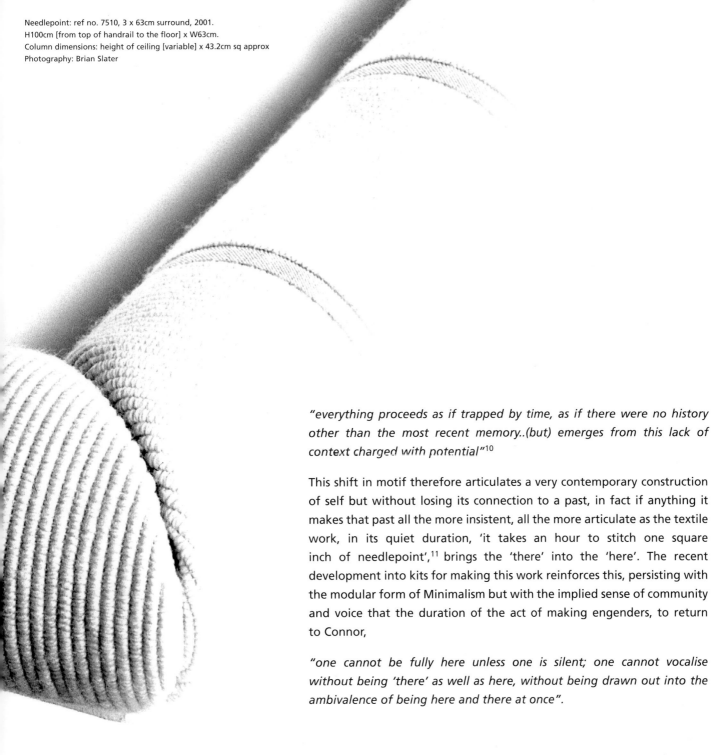

Needlepoint: ref no. 7510, 3 x 63cm surround, 2001.
H100cm [from top of handrail to the floor] x W63cm.
Column dimensions: height of ceiling [variable] x 43.2cm sq approx
Photography: Brian Slater

"everything proceeds as if trapped by time, as if there were no history other than the most recent memory..(but) emerges from this lack of context charged with potential"[10]

This shift in motif therefore articulates a very contemporary construction of self but without losing its connection to a past, in fact if anything it makes that past all the more insistent, all the more articulate as the textile work, in its quiet duration, 'it takes an hour to stitch one square inch of needlepoint',[11] brings the 'there' into the 'here'. The recent development into kits for making this work reinforces this, persisting with the modular form of Minimalism but with the implied sense of community and voice that the duration of the act of making engenders, to return to Connor,

"one cannot be fully here unless one is silent; one cannot vocalise without being 'there' as well as here, without being drawn out into the ambivalence of being here and there at once".

Installation shot Light-switch ref: 203/18 2003
Dimensions variable
Photography: Peter Huggins, Camera Techniques

CLOTHING THE GRID: ALTERATIONS AND ALTERNATIONS

By Victoria Mitchell

INSERTING THE PANEL

Maxine Bristow's studio presents an ordered environment, reflecting a methodical manner of working. It is only when the initial encounter moves beyond the carefully stacked piles of completed work, samples, experiments and work in progress that the richness of these methods begins to unfold. What at first sight registers as complicity with the tenets of a measured and reasoned Modernity gives way, little by little, to reveal traces of disruption, displacement and complex encounter. Between the outward manifestation of structured order and the subtle textures of interiority, surfaces are revealed as layers, lines as folds or seams, and function (that bastion of industrial Modernity) is carefully but resolutely turned on its head. Industrious method is turned against the mechanistic intentions of mass-producing industries to reveal the voice of the *subject* that such industries have so insistently displaced.

In this sensitive but profound shift, the mediating agency is the engineering of textile and cloth, and in particular, the possibilities inherent in the considered re-working of the *panel* of cloth by means of which a succession of visual and critical dialogues is constructed, as between clothing and environment, subject voice and (dis)functional object, or between the intricate work of the needle and the (de)construction of the archetypical grid. The panel can be likened to the ground on which text is written, but it is also a text in itself. We are reminded that text denotes weaving, and that weaving lies at the origin of the panel. For all its subtlety of textures and colourings a rectangle of plain-woven cloth is a straightforward geometry of interwoven horizontal and vertical threads. When it is positioned flat against a wall or laid out level on a horizontal surface, the structure displays a further form of geometry as a *plane.* This plane/plain horizontal-vertical mesh or grid of alternating dimensions can also be described as a panel or pane; the English word 'pane' (from which panel is derived) originating in the Latin word *pannus*, meaning 'a piece of cloth'.

Even familiar non-textile associations, such as panes of glass and wooden panelling or the panel that serves as a jury or collective body of discussants, refer back to the humble panel of cloth. The different references of each have affinity with the plane/plain construction of cloth through the rectangular, regulating division of, or within, a surface: a formation of compartments added together or laid out side by side. Regular and regulating across a broad stretch of associations, the panel works not only as a phenomenon in its own right but also a material surface or ground for some other activity, such as embroidery, painting, engraving, writing or, as in the work of Bristow, surfacing with gesso or embedding with needle work.[1]

Typically, panels are *insertions*, nestling into a frame or surrounding fixture. With her large panel-bags and hangings Bristow has released the panel from the inevitability of this framing, but she also draws attention to the insert, as in the bound buttonholes of her early work, or, more recently, in the interplay between panels of cloth and the insertions that are to be found in the fixtures and fittings of architecture, such as air vents, light switches and rails. This frees the panel from familiar contexts, and transposes the insert from one context to another, as from garment to grill or from metal to cloth. An alternation thus ensues between clothing and grid. Whereas things and objects in the world are typically perceived as cut off from one another, fragmenting perception, in this work, through a succession of *alterations* and *alternations*, objects open into dialogue with one another with the panel acting as intermediary.

The rectangular panel returns again and again as *leitmotif* in Bristow's work, as an iterative refrain, always moving against the iconic gestures of a singular, closed reading. Readings shift equivocally, from intimations of abstract geometries through details of clothing, engineering and furnishing to matters of embodiment and identity. Frequently interlined

TOP
Light-switch ref: 203/18 2003
Dimensions variable
Photography: Peter Huggins, Camera Techniques

BOTTOM
Conduit ref: 203/18 [Detail] 2003
Dimensions variable
Photography: Damian Chapman and Ian Forsyth

and interfaced, these panels suggest a trace of association with the 'counterpane'.[2] Through wadding and padding held together by the stitching of its outer layers the counterpane cushions the body from above as it drifts between worlds. Insertion gives way to incorporation, a term of embodiment. The panel used in this way may signal an embodiment of the grid, and of modernity.

INVESTING THE EVERYDAY

Becoming is what enables a trait, a line, an orientation, an event to be released from the system, series, organism or object that may have the effect of transforming the whole, making it no longer function singularly: it is an encounter between bodies that releases something from each and, in the process, releases or makes real a virtuality, a series of enabling and transforming possibilities.[3]

However abstract, virtual, complex or poetic in Bristow's art, there is invariably something recognizable and ordinary, a reminder of everyday functions, of objects that are easily named, or familiar actions of the sort we take for granted. These functional references, displaced or transformed through the artwork in the sense suggested by Elizabeth Grosz, means that they no longer function 'singularly' and often focus our attention on details. This is not a crude 'cutting out' of details from their familiar functions but a subtle crafting of associations, a sustained enquiry that relishes the play of signifiers as they mark the passage from the certain logic of inevitable reality to poetic and critical engagement.

The activity of making is the agency of change, a means for manipulating the transformation of meaning: an active positioning which is also political. This is prescient. As Grosz concludes, 'what is now in question is the making of things, and that from which things are made. This is what the rigorous process of intuition draws us toward, not things themselves so much as the teeming, suffuse network within which things are formed and outlined, the flux of the real'.[4] Such 'things' as button holes, bags, light switches and air vents are subject to a shuttling from one network in

Conduit ref: 203/18 2003
Dimensions variable
Photography: Peter Huggins, Camera Techniques

Doing Without: Sustaining 7 Square Metres 1999
Overall dimensions: H163cmxW418cm
Individual pieces: H163cmxW124cm
Photography: Dewi Tannatt Lloyd

which they are embedded unobtrusively to another in which they are staged within the shared arena of display and discourse.

Cloth and clothing carry phenomenological and psychological resonance through this wresting of the poetic from the functional. 'The thing and the body are correlates' says Grosz. 'The thing is "made" for the body….manipulable for the body's needs'.[5] Thus the relationship between bodies and things is formative and negotiable through the technology of making that ensures 'the deepening investment of the one, the body, in the other, the thing'.[6] The notion of investment is particularly poignant, suggestive as it is of clothing and covering as garment. To borrow a term from tailoring, Bristow's body of work forms an *interface* between the body and the thing, thus taking the in-between of the garment as the panelling which embeds and inserts the disparity of things and their overlooked details into an ordered account.

In one register, Bristow plays on the interface between the 'engineering' of hand and machine revealing the possibilities of porosity and at the same time measured exchange between the two. In a related orchestration of difference there is a focus on relationships between the one, the several and the many; singularity is pinpointed, but only to be released through multiplication, repetition and series. This detailing in the making, repeated as if to reference the eternal return of the same, compels our attention to the otherwise overlooked details of the everyday. Caught between fixture and detachment, proximity and distance, measured familiarity and the infinity of the unknown, buttonholes and air vents are revealed not as different 'objects' but as part of a continuum or flux, traversing the boundaries of their singularity.

'Objects', suggests Donna Harraway, are 'boundary projects' which 'shift from within'.[7] Thus a bag may carry intimations of dialogue between the body and objects in the world, or between concealment of a hidden interior and openness to visual scrutiny. For Bristow the concealment associated with the hidden interior of the bags is latent in the formation and serried presentation of the panels from which they are formed, their

25

deep interiors hidden from view, glimpsed only through the open ends. The weight and sag of the hanging bag carries intimations of the body. In his seminal essay 'The Poetics of Softness' (1967), the critic Max Kosloff said that 'regardless of how abstract a soft sculpture is, it will unavoidably evoke the human'. He describes relationships between bodies and sculptures as always 'revealing', but suggests that whereas the typically solid materials of sculpture tend to effect a formal abstract or aesthetic response, the yielding and somatic surface of 'an object becalmed' through softness is more likely to be interpreted through metaphor.[8] Bristow's object-forms conceal and exceed their functional association in equivocal fashion allowing the conversation between material and function to carry the metaphorical load.

Against the abstraction and regulation of cloth's formal geometry, and yet always in some kind of alternating play or exchanging dialogue with the grids of its construction, the becalmed and becalming object-forms which have become the hallmark of Bristow's work over the past ten years both yield to cloth's inherent pliability and yet at the same time evoke a restraint which prevents the yielding from collapse and deformation. Reference to bodily comfort is revealed not through some kind of release from the everyday into the collapsed landscape of a dream or a comic interior, but rather through the quiet contemplation of the boundaries across which the relationship between the everyday and the psyche shuttles to and fro, as if caught in a continuous ribbon of subtle displacements and turns.

The recurring object-world of her attention is characterised by a play of restraint and openness, a negotiating and detailing of entrance and egress, aperture and closure, barrier and vent. There is a reiteration of access, or access denied. Boundaries are potent sites of transformation, transgression and transition, restraining forces or impediments, to be negotiated if they are to be overcome. They not only touch on the functional but also mark the liminal, thresholds not only of the architectural and physical but also the psychological domain. For Martin Heidegger 'a boundary is not that at which something stops but ... is that

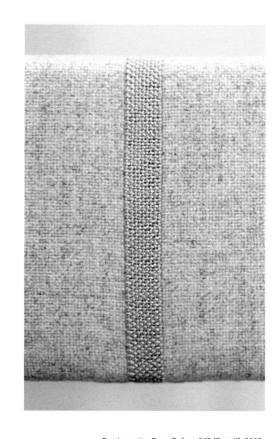

Barrier units: Darn Ref no.648 [Detail], 2005
Individual units: H89cm x W24cm x L208cm
Photography: Maxine Bristow

Barrier units: Darn Ref no.648, 2005
Individual units: H89cm x W24cm x L208cm
Photography: Maxine Bristow

from which something begins its presencing', thus a potent place from which it is possible to reflect on what has gone before and on what is, for Grosz, a 'becoming'.[9] For Bristow, the activity of *making* is instrumental as a form of becoming, a succession of alterations and alternations that refuse closure.

ACUITY AND REPARATION OF HABIT

Making is a particular preoccupation of the crafts, and although often identified as anachronistic, Bristow resists the closure that would silence the time-honoured skills and knowledge associated with the activity of the 'maker'. Paradoxically, this is effected in one register of representation through a focus on the habitual and repetitive skills which presage to a significant extent the loss of status of the artisan. However repetition is not only an anchor of the industrious maker; it is also the work of the subject who makes, in contrast to the hegemonic propensity of measure and reason. Within visual practice, repetition works against the grain of the iconic to signal difference (that 'teeming, suffuse network' of which Grosz speaks, or the richly textured effects of surface in Bristow's work) as well as similitude.

The tailor (to reference skills from which Bristow draws) who cuts and measures 'according to the cloth' in order to fit the body and to fashion transformations and identities is concerned with *detail* in the relationship between measure and cloth, precisely, as suggested by the French word *détailler*, (from LL. *taliare*, to cut), that is, the cutting of cloth into pieces or 'details'. For Bristow, tailoring skills are far removed from the rhetoric of fashion, but they are not in consequence to be entirely disregarded. There are parallels to be drawn between the detailing of the tailor or seamstress and that of the architect or engineer who designs and makes a 'fitting' for a wall or window. Her medium may be textile but the skills have wider reference.

Materially it is the detailed and repetitive work of the *stitch* (of both hand and machine) which provides the syntax on which the ordering of concepts depends. The stitch draws through the cloth as if puncturing a boundary between past and present, or negotiating a relationship between the invisible and visible. The stitch constructs, but it also repairs that which is worn out through excessive use. It signals dependence upon a repetition inscribed both in necessity and in contemplation, the latter as if marking the rhythms of time and duration while steering a passage between fatigue and dream. Together in the act of sewing, needle and thread are the agents of an intimate conversation between eye/ hand/ mind. In this they share something with pen and ink (or their contemporary equivalent), leaving traces of their engagement with every mark, formative of a language to be shared and then critically deciphered. To be 'as sharp as a needle' is to have acuity, (L. *acus*, needle) whether of wit, vision or skill. Against the model example of the Victorian child, trained to accomplish mastery in the matter of plain sewing so as to engage dutifully in the needs of household management, the work of Bristow has broken rank and violated convention, needling with acuity the flesh of patriarchy.

The needle is a hard, sharp tool, at times cruel, as in pricking fingers, endangering eyes or painfully breaking skin in the repeated rubbing of the needle into the flesh of the fingertips. Readings of this very small item with its even smaller aperture are coloured by intimations of difficulty and discomfort, as in the futile search for the (proverbial) needle in a haystack, the uncomfortable psychological implications of being irritated, or 'needled' and the unpleasant physical sensations of 'pins and needles'. The *wear* of 'wear and tear' is potent and poignant with meaning. Thus we wear a garment but it becomes worn through use. As a result of incessant sewing the maker of the garment might also be worn out, or as in the case of a certain tailor of Gloucester, 'worn to a ravelling'. The skills of 'needle work' themselves take their toll on the body and psyche, demanding a concentrated eye, a constantly steady hand, and in the case of Victorian sewing instruction, the probability of tedium.

Inserting a gusset or band, scalloping, binding, piping, tucks, seams, openings, grafting, patching and darning all had their place in the

Square Correlation No. 2 1999]
Dimensions: H74cmxW150cm
Photography: Maxine Bristow

 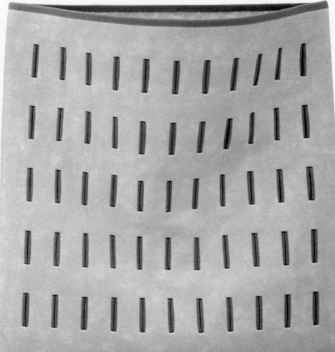

domestic economy. With the passage of a supple thread through the eye of a metallic needle countless generations of infants and young children were initiated into the drill of 'needle work'.[10] It was from her seamstress grandmother and home dressmaker mother that Bristow learned the skills of this meticulous and intimate engineering without which all manner of stuff (material and social) would fall apart. Such histories pervade the everyday environment, evidence of the legacy of sewing as an act of endurance, obedience, thrift and, in surmounting these, a sense of pleasure.

The work of the needle carries notions of reparation, a making good not only in the thing to be repaired but also in the endless cycle of reparation in a figurative or conceptual sense.[11] For the philosopher Gilles Deleuze,

repetition (as in the stitches without end in the incessant making of useful things) and habit inform one another, begetting a 'thousand intertwinings' with which 'difference inhabits repetition'.[12] As with wear and tear, notions of habit suggest a psychological incorporation of ingrained clothing, an article of clothing (a habit) informed by a pattern of being, and of being in or *inhabiting* the world. Deleuze considers that 'in every way, material or bare repetition, so called repetition of the same, is like a skin which unravels, the external husk of a kernel of difference and more complicated internal repetitions'.[13] It is as if in every doing there is an undoing, in every constructing an unravelling, in every act of cutting-out in preparation for constructing there is a comparable cutting-out of material beneath the threshold of conscious knowledge or visibility.

In Bristow's methodical lines of stitches (or the removal of threads) and measured panels it is as if repetition itself has become porous, or inhabited. As one series (or line) ends another begins, each repetitive mark opening out into and informing the next, reinforcing the habitual return of the same as a activity of contemplation and security as well as an unravelling of an interior world. The very instability, outwardly, of Bristow's object-things (and the impossibility of giving them a name) masks a security founded on such inhabiting. For Deleuze habit is the foundation of time which depends, through repetition, on memory. Thus stitch, panel and cloth are embedded in and through a reworking of the invisible (histories) which memory enfolds in the act of making.

REDRESSING MODERNITY

Within the memories that are revealed and questioned through Bristow's explorations, there is reference to the history of Modernism. I began by suggesting that the panel acts as an agency of modernity, with its horizontal-vertical interpenetrations and planar surfaces likened to a weave. In the ordered and methodical working of Bristow's studio it is possible to glimpse the logic of the discipline which Mark Wrigley, recalling Adolf Loos, might align with the correctness of the well-cut suit.[14] The suit begets the office, and vice versa, as if each has its place on

Darn: ref no. 648, 3 x 146 cm division, 2002 [Detail]
H100cm x W 146cm approx [space between columns variable]
Photography: Sara Morris

that transparent emblem of modernity, the grid. But the grid itself, as recalled and deconstructed by the critic Rosalind Krauss in the light of the structural analysis of myth, can also be subject to narratives of the psyche.[15] In the intense and private work of the artist Eva Hesse such as *Accretion* and *Augment/Aught* of 1968, rectangular panels of canvas painted with latex are sewn together so that they billow and sag. Latex for Hesse functions as a 'barely something' that brings the sensitivity of touch to the impersonal dryness of optical reason.

In Bristow's recent work there is a reminder of this reclamation of sight through touch in *Double-lined* (198x82), an extensive series of panels hung over rails, framing the bare white walls of a gallery. Each panel of striped fabric is padded and stitched in the manner of a counterpane, drawing attention in the hanging to the pensive weight of construction in contrast to, and at one remove from, the dressed white skin of the walls. In a further accretion of tactility the panels are rubbed and pounded, from edge to edge, with gesso. There is a rawness here that Hesse would have understood but which would have been an anathema to architects of modernity such as Loos. Yet the work is in intimate alternation with the functional architecture against which it is turned and by which it is framed. As consistent with all her previous work Bristow continues here to articulate the crafted intimacy of subject positions against a context of blind authority and uniformity. Whereas the work of Donald Judd (to which Bristow has referred) could be described as 'furnishing' the grid, Bristow's work may be said to clothe it, without losing sight of the detailing that make all the difference.

Barrier ref 1: 9774/14, 2003
H91cm x L165cm x W41cm
Photography: Peter Huggins, Camera Techniques

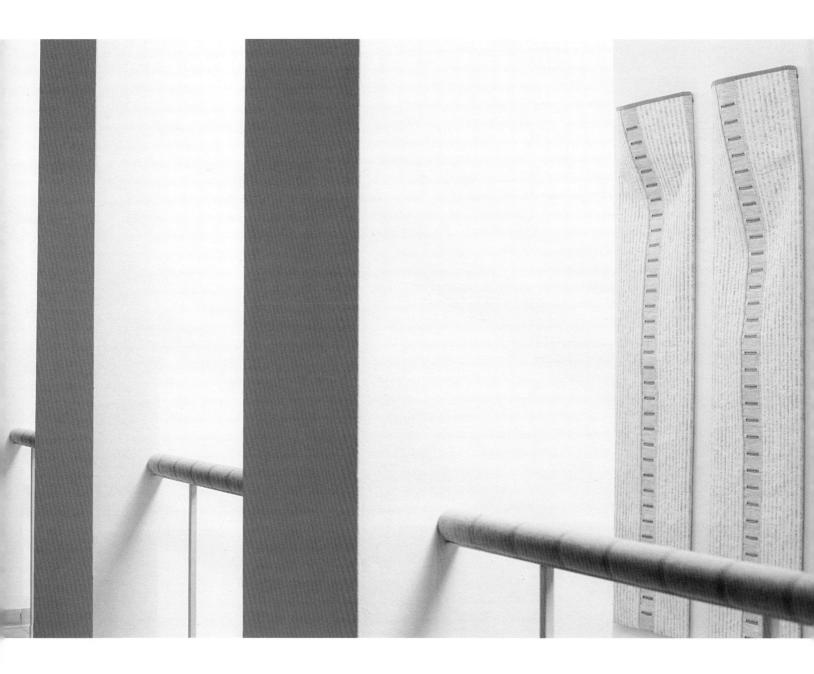

Installation shot, Jerwood Applied Arts Prize 2002: Textiles
Includes:
18 x 51 over 11.44
Darn: ref no. 648, 3 x 146 cm division
Photography: Maxine Bristow

NOTES AND REFERENCES

Essay by Elisa Oliver

[1] Steven Connor, 'The Strains of the Voice' essay written to accompany the exhibition Phonorama: *Eine Kulturgeschichte der Stimme als Medium*, curated by Brigitte Felderer, at the Zentrum für Kunst und Medientechnologie, Karlsruhe, 18 September 2004 - 30 January 2005.

[2] Conversation with the artist May 2006.

[3] Of particular interest to the artist was Marsha Meskimmon's Engendering the *City Woman Artists and Urban Space*, Scarlet Press 1997.

[4] Maxine Bristow *Material Trace-Marking Time and Defining Space, Catalogue essay Through the Surface: Collaborating Textile Artists From Britain and Japan* January 2003.

[5] Psychoanalytic term/idea developed by Freud (1925) literally means 'un-homely' see *The Psychological Works of Sigmund Freud*, James Strachey (ed) Vintage 2001.

[6] Nina Saunders is a British artist who came to prominence in the 1990s with a trademark transformation of chairs and sofas through large upholstered bulbous protrusions.

[7] see Wendy Wheeler 'Nostalgia isn't Nasty-the Postmodernising of Parliamentary Democracy' in Mark Perryman (ed.) *Altered States: Postmodernism, Politics, Culture* London: Lawrence and Wishart 1994.

[8] For a definition of non-place see Marc Augè Non-Places: *Introduction to an Anthropology of Supermodernity*, London, Verso 1995.

[9] Soo Jin Kim' Uta Barth, The Place of Non-Place', Claustrophobia, Exhibition Catalogue Ikon Gallery Birmingham 1998.

[10] Opcit 9

[11] Maxine Bristow *Revealed*, Catalogue essay, Nottingham Castle Museum and Art Gallery, September 2005.

Essay by Victoria Mitchell

[1] Small panels or pieces of parchment were used in the seventeenth and eighteenth century to enter the names of a jury, hence the panel as the jury itself.

[2] 'Counterpane' is more complicated than it seems at first, having links not only with pane through (L.) *pannus* but also with two other derivations: the French *contrepointe* and *cuilte* point, (with the 'pointle' deriving from the Latin *punctum*, prick) and the Latin *culcita puncta*, a quilted mattress or cushion. In these cases the *pointe* and *punctum* both refer to the pricks and stitches of sewing rather than the panels that (may) make up the whole. But with links of *contrepointe* to 'counterpoint' (as used, for example, in music) there may also be a sense in which matching (opposite, counter) panels are brought together, as is the case in so many quilts and counterpanes. At some stage, the *pannus* and *puctum* derivations fuse into a single (quilted) counterpane.

[3] Elizabeth Grosz, *Architecture from the Outside* (Cambridge, Massachusetts, London, England, The MIT Press), p.70.

[4] Grosz, op.cit. p.179.

[5] Ibid. p.182.

[6] Ibid.

[7] Donna Harraway, *Simians, Cyborgs* and *Women*, (London, Free Association of Books), p.201, quoted by Marsha Meskimmon, *Women Making Art*, (London and New York, Routledge), p.85.

[8] Max Kosloff, 'The Poetics of Softness', from the catalogue of the exhibition 'American Sculpture of the Sixties', LACMA, 1967, reprinted in *Renderings* (London, Studio Vista, 1970), p.224. The essay brilliantly deconstructs Claes Oldenburg's 'comatose' objects.

[9] Martin Heidegger 'Building, Dwelling, Thinking' in *Poetry, Language, Thought,* translated by Albert Hofstadter,(New York, Harper and Row, 1975), p.154.

[10] If Agnes Walker, writing in 1897, is to be believed, 'needle drill', using a coarse carpet needle and twine, is recommended for 'Babies or Lower Class of Infants'. Agnes Walker *Manual of Needle Work and Cutting Out*, (London, Blackie and Sons, Third Edition 1902), p.7.

[11] As in the writings of Melanie Klein.

[12] Gilles Deleuze, *Difference and Repetition*, translated by Paul Patton, (London and New York, Continuum, 2001), pp76-77.

[13] Ibid. p.76.

[14] Mark Wigley, *White Walls, Designer Dresses: The Fashioning of Modern Architecture*, (Cambridge, Massachusetts, London, England, The MIT Press), p.111.

[15] Rosalind Krauss 'Grids, You Say', catalogue essay to accompany *Grids* (New York, Pace Gallery, Dec.1978 – Jan.1979).

MAXINE BRISTOW

Personal Details:

Name: Maxine Bristow
Address: 5 Tilston Road, Malpas, Cheshire, SY14 7DB
Tel: Home: 01948 860065, Work: 01244 513030
Fax: 01244 511300
e mail: m.bristow@chester.ac.uk

Qualifications:

1985   MA Textiles, Manchester Metropolitan University [formerly polytechnic]
1984   BA [Hons] Fashion/Textiles [Embroidery], First Class Honours
              Manchester Metropolitan University [formerly polytechnic]
1981   Foundation in Art and Design, Bolton College of Art

Teaching Experience and Employment:

2004 - Present   Reader in Fine Art, MA Fine Art Programme Leader, University of Chester
1993 - 2004   Senior Lecturer, Department of Fine Art, University College Chester
                 BA [Hons] Fine Art, BA [Hons] Combined Studies,
                 Joint Co-ordinator MA Fine Art
1989 - 1993   Part-time Lecturer, Department of Fine Art, University College Chester
1988 - 1989   Freelance Designer [Furnishings]
1986 - 1988   Artist in Residence/Art Teacher/Freelance Designer
                 Heathfield School for Girls, 11-18yrs, Ascot, Berkshire

Visiting Lecturer:

1999   University of Ulster, Belfast
1998   Goldsmiths College, London
1987   Norwich School of Art and Design
1986/87/88   Chesterfield College of Art and Technology

External Examiner:

2005 - 2008   BA [Hons] Textiles, Fashion and Fibre, Winchester School of Art,
              University of Southampton
2005 - 2008   BA [Hons] Applied Arts, University of Hertfordshire
2004 - 2006   MA Art and Design, University of Luton
2000 - 2005   BA [Hons] Textile Crafts, University of Huddersfield

Solo Exhibitions:

2004   Serial Repetition Grosvenor Museum, Chester.
1999   Southern Arts Touring Exhibition Service. Maidstone Library Gallery.
1999   Kunstindustrimuseum, Copenhagen.
1997   Southern Arts Touring Exhibition Service. Banbury Museum, Oxfordshire;
              Viables Craft Centre, Basingstoke; The Winchester Gallery, Hampshire.

Group Exhibitions:

2005   Reveal, Nottingham Museum and Art Gallery
              Hands Across the Border. Ruthin Craft Centre; The Hub, Sleaford; Mission
              Gallery, Swansea: The Black Swan Gallery, Frome.
2004/2005   Through the Surface, Collaborating Textile Artists from Britain and Japan.
              James Hockey and Foyer Galleries, The Surrey Institute of Art & Design
              University College, Farnham; Brighton and Hove Museum and Art Gallery; The
              Sainsbury Centre for Visual Art, Norwich; Bankfield Museum,
              Huddersfield, and Piece Hall, Halifax; Nottingham Castle Museum and Art
              Gallery; Kyoto Museum of Modern Art, Kyoto.
2002   The Gaps Between, International Textile Biannual 2002. Ormeau Baths
              Gallery, Belfast.

	Jerwood Applied Arts Prize 2002: Textiles. Crafts Council, London; Salford Museum and Art Gallery, Manchester; Crafts Council of Ireland, Kilkenny; Ulster Museum, Belfast.
2001	The 10th International Triennial of Tapestry. Museum of Textiles, Lodz, Poland.
	Dovetail. Travelling Gallery, City Art Centre, Edinburgh.
2000	The Contemplative Stitch. H&R Block Artspace at The Kansas City Art Institute, USA.
1999	The 6th International Textile Competition '99 - Kyoto. Museum of Kyoto, Japan.
	[Un] Limited. Diversity and Change in International Contemporary Craft. Crafts Council, London.
	Textures of Memory: The Poetics of Cloth. Angel Row Gallery, Nottingham; Pittshanger Gallery, London; Piece Hall, Halifax; MAC, Birmingham.
1998	Knot as They Seam: Puns and Permutations in Fibre Arts. Maryland Art Place, Baltimore, USA.
	Contemporary Embroidery: An International Perspective. The Arts Centre at Dockland, Bermuda.
	Joint exhibition with Claire Curneen. MAC, Birmingham.
	Stitch. Bury St. Edmunds Art Gallery.
	Natural Resources. Ruthin Crafts Centre, Oriel 31, Newtown.
1997	Flexible 2 Pan European Art. Nederland Textielmuseum, Tilburg, Netherlands; Galeria Awangarda, Wroclaw, Poland; Whitworth Art Gallery, Manchester, Great Britain.
	British Art Textiles. Bury St. Edmunds Art Gallery; Watermans Art Centre, Brentford; Mercer Art Gallery, Harrogate; Braintree District Museum, Bonnington Gallery, Nottingham; Orleans Hose Gallery, Twickenham; MAC, Birmingham; Durham Art Gallery.
	Leinen. Galerie Handwerk, Munich, Germany.

Collections:

• Crafts Council, London.
• Whitworth Art Gallery, Manchester.
• 'Doing Without: Sustaining 7 Square Metres' purchased by the Contemporary Art Society Special Collection Scheme on behalf of Nottingham Castle Museum & Art Gallery with funds from the Arts Council Lottery, 2003.
• Collaborative piece 'Pockets/Ventillation Grill' [produced as an outcome of Through the Surface, Collaborating Textile Artists from Britain and Japan] purchased by the Contemporary Art Society Special Collection Scheme on behalf of Nottingham Castle Museum & Art Gallery with funds from the Arts Council Lottery, 2004.

Professional Membership/Esteem indicators/Awards:

• Nomination by one of the HE subject associations and subsequent invitation to serve as a member on sub-panel 63 in the 2008 Research Assessment Exercise.
• Co Director, Centre for Practice as Research in the Arts [CPaRA], University of Chester.
• 2004-2007 Member of Photostore Selected Makers Panel, Crafts Council, London
• Member North West Textile Forum.
• Member North West Art and Design Research Group.
• One of 3 established UK artists selected to mentor emerging Japanese artists as part of Through the Surface, Collaborating Textile Artists from Britain and Japan, 2003.
• Selected for BBC production Contemporary Visions, a series of short films profiling 8 contemporary artists including Turner Prize winner Grayson Perry, Fiona Rae, Laura Ford, Martin Parr, Learning Zone, December 2003
• Shortlisted for the Jerwood Applied Arts Prize 2002: Textiles. Crafts Council, London.
• One of Four artists selected to represent Great Britain at The 10th International Triennial of Tapestry. Museum of Textiles, Lodz, Poland, 2001.
• Northwest Arts Individual Development Grant, 2000.
• British Council Grant, 2000.

Publications-Catalogues:

- Revealed. Forward by Kate Stoddard, Introductory essay by Dr Jennifer Harris. Essay on works in the collection [Doing Without: Sustaining 7 Square Metres, 2003, and Pockets/Ventilation Grill, 2004] by Maxine Bristow and Lesley Millar respectively. Nottingham Museum and Art Gallery, 2005. ISBN 0 905634 72
- Hands Across the Border. Introduction by Philip Hughes, essays by Amanda Fielding and Judy Dames. Ruthin Craft Centre, 2004. ISBN 1 900941 77 5
- Through the Surface Collaborating Textile Artists from Britain and Japan. Introductions by Ian Dumelow and Takeo Uchiyama; foreword Professor Marie Conte-Helm; essays by Lesley Millar, Keiko Kawashima, Jay Merrick, Gerry Diebel, and the 14 project artists. The Surrey Institute of Art and Design, 2004. ISBN 0-9546285-2-7
- Jerwood Applied Arts Prize 2002: Textiles. Essay by Lesley Millar. Crafts Council, London, 2002ISBN 1-903713-07-2.
- The Gaps Between, International Textile Biannual 2002. Essay by David Brett. Ormeau Baths Gallery, Belfast, 2003.
- The 10th International Triennial of Tapestry. Introduction by Norbert Zawiskza, essay by Irena Huml. Museum of Textiles, Lodz, Poland, 2001. ISBN 83-913224-0-8.
- Textures of Memory: The Poetics of Cloth. Essays by Pamela Johnson and Pennina Barnett. Angel Row Gallery, Nottingham, 1999. ISBN 0 905 634 39X.
- [Un] Limited. Repetition and Change in International Contemporary Craft. Foreword by Dr Louise Taylor, introduction by Emmanuel Cooper, and essay by John Tozer. Crafts Council, London, 1999. ISBN 1 870145 85 2.
- The 6th International Textile Competition '99 - Kyoto. Museum of Kyoto, Japan.
- Natural Resources. Ruthin Crafts Centre, 1998. ISBN 1 9000 941 14 7.
- Knot as They Seam: Puns and Permutations in Fibre Arts. Maryland Art Place, Baltimore, USA.
- Catalogue to accompany solo show. Essay by John Gillet. Southern Arts Touring, 1997. ISBN 1 873451 31 8.
- British Art Textiles. Foreword by Barbara Taylor, essays by Linda Theophilus and Judith Ellen Duffey [Harding]. Bury St. Edmunds Art Gallery, 1996. ISBN 0 9528639 0 1.
- Flexible 2 Pan European Art. Nederlands Textielmuseum, Tilburg, 1996. ISBN 90-70962-27-6.

Publications-papers/essays

- 'Maxine Bristow', catalogue essay in Revealed, Nottingham Castle Museum and Art Gallery, 2005. pp.38-39 ISBN 0 905634 72
- Exhibition Review, 'Surfacing: Retrospective and New Work by Polly Binns' in Textile, Volume 2, Issue 2, pp.208-217. Berg, 2004. ISSN1475-9756/ISBN 1 85973 759 5
- 'Material Trace-Marking Time and Defining Space' in Through the Surface Collaborating Textile Artists from Britain and Japan, p.58-59. The Surrey Institute of Art and Design, 2004. ISBN 0-9546285-2-7
- Journal documenting contribution to Through the Surface Collaborating Textile Artists from Britain and Japan published at www.throughthesurface.surrart.ac.uk.
- 'Three Weeks to Turn 348, Three Years to Turn Intuition Towards Understanding' in Ideas in The Making: Practice in Theory, 1998. University of East Anglia/Crafts Council. ISBN 187014581X.
- 'Material Culture - The Language of Textiles' in The World of Embroidery, p.308-310, vol.48. no.6, November, 1997. ISSN 1351-9603.

Conference/Symposium presentations:

- Breakout group leader Ambiguous Spaces, symposium to accompany the exhibition 2121 The Textile vision of Reiko Sudo and Nuno, University College for the Creative Arts at Farnham, 11.11.05
- Joint presentation with Kyoko Nitta, Through the Surface Symposium, Museum of Modern Art, Kyoto, Japan, 22.04.05
- Conference presentation - Creative Dates. A Conference of the North West Art and Design Research Group, 23-24.09.04
- Joint convenor, What's in the Tin? Research Symposium to mark the launch of the Centre for

Practice as Research in the Arts, University College Chester, 27.10.04
- Keynote speaker, Textile Symposium, Celebrating Diversity in Stitch, Ruthin Craft Centre, 2.10.04
- Seminar - Creative Dialogues 2 [joint presentation with Kyoko Nitta as part of Through the Surface, Collaborating Textile Artists from Britain and Japan], Bankfield Museum and Art Gallery, Halifax, 23.7.04
- Keynote speaker, Cheshire Annual Art and Design Conference, Frodsham, Cheshire, 17.01.04
- Seminar presentation, Textile Vocabularies, Innovation in Practice. 29.10.03, Herriot Watt University, Scottish Borders Campus, Galashiels
- Seminar presentation, Jerwood Applied Arts Prize 2002: Textiles. Crafts Council, London, 21.10.02.
- 'Mapping Territories - Defining Contexts', Nomansland Conference, Bath City College, 23.3.02.
- Kon'texst Locating and Developing Practice, seminar convenor and presentation of paper, Chester College of Higher Education, 6.10.01.
- 'Exchanging the Planks' seminar presentation at Textile Forum, Knowle House, Sevenoaks, [Organised by Kent County Council and chaired by Professor Anne Morrell], 5.5.98.
- 'Three Weeks to Turn 348, Three Years to Turn Intuition Towards Understanding', Ideas in The Making: Practice in Theory, conference presentation, University of East Anglia/Crafts Council, 25.4.98.
- Textile Matters - a public debate on issues surrounding the production and status of contemporary art. Whitworth Art Gallery, Manchester, [Chaired by Jennifer Harris as part of a programme of event accompanying Flexible 2: Pan European Art], May 1997

Reviews/Articles/Citations:

- Kay Greenlees, 'Revealed: Nottingham's Contemporary Textiles' in Selvedge, Nov/Dec 05, Issue 08, p. 88. ISSN 1742-254X
- Jessica Hemmings, 'A Bridge Between Britain and Japan' in Surface Design Journal, pp.36-41, Fall 2004.
- Oliver Lowenstein, 'Through the Surface' in FibreArts, p.46-51, Sept/October 2004.
- Lesley Millar, 'Through the Surface' in a-n Magazine, p.32-35, April 2004.
- Liz Hoggard, 'Surface Treatment' in Crafts, no. 187, pp.25-31, March/April 2004.
- Hilary Turner, 'Through the Surface: Collaboration, Process and Outcome' in Journal for Weavers, Spinners and Dyers, pp.20-24, March 2004.
- Angela Kennedy, 'Fabric Futures' in IdFX Magazine, p.34-39, March 2004.
- Polly Leonard, 'Through the Surface Collaborating Textile Artists from Britain and Japan' in Embroidery vol.54, pp.38-39 Sept 2003.
- Polly Binns, 'Jerwood Applied Arts Prize' in Textile - The Journal of Cloth and Culture, vol.1, issue 1, Spring 2003.
- Mary Schoeser, 'Jerwood Applied Arts Prize 2002: Textiles' in Crafts, no.180 Jan/Feb 2003, p.50
- Jo Saunders, 'Jerwood Applied Arts Prize 2002: Textiles' in Embroidery, vol.54, Jan 2003
- Polly Leonard, 'Textile Innovation The Jerwood Prize for Textiles' in Embroidery Magazine, September 2002, pp.20-21
- Anne Hamlyn, 'Textures of Memory' in n.paradoxa Vol.6, 2000. ISSN 1461-0434
- 'Textures of Memory the Poetics of Cloth' in Crafts, no.162, Jan/Feb 2000
- Polly Leonard, 'Cloth or Concept Trends in Textiles Today' in The World of Embroidery, July 1998 Volume 49, No.4
- Pamela Johnson, 'A Sense of Order', Crafts, vol. 47 July/August 1997, p.26-29. ISSN 0306-6 10x
- Pamela Johnson, exhibition review Flexible 2, Crafts, vol. 47 July/August 1997, pp.53-54. ISSN 0306-6 10x
- Pamela Johnson, 'Time for Textiles', Crafts, No.144 January/February 1997, pp.20-25. ISSN 0306-610X.
- Renata Brink, 'Textile Texts' in Artists Newsletter, November 1996.

ACKNOWLEDGEMENTS

Bolton Museum opened in 1884 as one of the first fully professional public museums. Housing Art, Egyptology, Archaeology, Industrial History and Natural History collections the museum has been at its current site since 1938.

The museum's temporary exhibition gallery shows a changing programme of exhibitions aiming to promote the work of local artists and strengthen the local arts infrastructure; display exhibitions relevant to and including the museum's collections; exhibit a range of art forms, presented at their highest quality. The *sensual austerity* exhibition enables Bolton Museum to fulfil two of these aims. Maxine was born and educated in Bolton and is now an established artist with an international reputation producing work of outstanding quality.

We welcome Maxine back to her home town and are proud to be able to celebrate her achievements. We hope that this exhibition will inspire young artists studying in Bolton today.

Bolton Museum is also pleased to have been able to work in partnership with The Hub, an internationally recognised centre for craft and design. As Maxine is presenting the exhibition differently in each space, we are excited to see how the show will evolve between the two contrasting venues.

I would like to take this opportunity to thank the many people whose hard work and support has made this project possible. First and foremost, Maxine, whose drive, determination and professionalism has ensured that an exceptional exhibition has been created. Thanks to Elisa Oliver and Victoria Mitchell for their insightful and inspiring contributions towards this publication. I would also like to thank Claire Phillips for all her work at The Hub throughout the development of the exhibition and Melanie Kidd and Phil Cosker for steering the exhibition through the final production stages. At Bolton Museum I would like to thank Liz Shaw, Miriam Moritz and Perry Bonewell for all their help and support. Maxine would personally like to extend her thanks to the Chester student 'gesso cracking team' – Lara, Anna, Sara, Nicola, Rebecca, Jo, and Helen, for their willingness and stamina. Many thanks also go to Kvadrat Ltd and Olicana Textiles for their sponsorship towards the cost of fabric and to T. Saveker and Stockport Sheet Metal Ltd for their sponsorship towards the metal fabrication. Last and not least thanks to the University of Chester and the Arts Council, England for their financial support.

Sarah Teale
Exhibitions Officer, Bolton Museum, Art Gallery and Aqaurium

156 Down 6 Side Seams.
Overall dimensions:H119cmxW416cm
Individual pieces: H119cmxW122cm
Photography: James Newell